Hello, America!

Colonial Williamsburg

by Kaitlyn Duling

Bullfrog Books

Ideas for Parents and Teachers

Bullfrog Books let children practice reading informational text at the earliest reading levels. Repetition, familiar words, and photo labels support early readers.

Before Reading

- Discuss the cover photo. What does it tell them?

- Look at the picture glossary together. Read and discuss the words.

Read the Book

- "Walk" through the book and look at the photos. Let the child ask questions. Point out the photo labels.

- Read the book to the child, or have him or her read independently.

After Reading

- Prompt the child to think more. Ask: If you visited Colonial Williamsburg, what part would you be most interested in seeing?

Bullfrog Books are published by Jump!
5357 Penn Avenue South
Minneapolis, MN 55419
www.jumplibrary.com

Library of Congress Cataloging-in-Publication Data

Names: Duling, Kaitlyn, author.
Title: Colonial Williamsburg / by Kaitlyn Duling.
Description: Bullfrog books edition.
Minneapolis, MN: Jump!, Inc., [2018]
Series: Hello, America! | Includes index.
Audience: Grades K-3. | Audience: Age 5-8.
Identifiers: LCCN 2017026372 (print)
LCCN 2017026091 (ebook)
ISBN 9781624966569 (e-book)
ISBN 9781620318607 (hard cover: alk. paper)
Subjects: LCSH: Colonial Williamsburg (Williamsburg, Va.)—Juvenile literature.
Williamsburg (Va.)—Juvenile literature. | Historic sites—Virginia—Williamsburg—Juvenile literature.
Classification: LCC F234.W7 (print)
LCC F234.W7 D85 2018 (ebook) | DDC 975.5/4252—dc23
LC record available at https://lccn.loc.gov/201702637

Editor: Kirsten Chang
Book Designer: Molly Ballanger
Photo Researcher: Molly Ballanger

Photo Credits: Zachary Frank/Alamy, cover; Bdphoto/iStock, 1, 22br; Dutourdumonde Photography/Shutterstock, 3; Roy Johnson/Alamy, 4; Sarah Hadley/Alamy, 5 (foreground); vgoodrich/iStock, 5 (background); Andre Jenny/Alamy, 6–7; jiawangkun/Shutterstock, 8–9; Jeff Greenberg/Alamy, 9; Mark Summerfield/Alamy, 10; Leigh Vogel/Stringer/Getty, 11; Michael Gordon/Shutterstock, 12–13; Irene Abdou/Alamy, 14–15, 22tl; D. Hurst/Alamy, 16–17, 20–21; martypatch/iStock, 18; netop2all/iStock, 19, 23bl; David Stuckel/Alamy, 22bl; Ritu Manoj Jethani/Shutterstock, 22tr; Perry Correll/Shutterstock, 23tl; Popartic/Dreamstime, 23tr (map); Cameramannz/Shutterstock, 23tr (pin); Viktor Kunz/Shutterstock, 23br; catnap72/iStock, 24.

Printed in the United States of America at Corporate Graphics in North Mankato, Minnesota.

Table of Contents

Living History

Welcome to Colonial Williamsburg.

Let's explore!

This town is old.

More than
200 years old!

It stays the same.

The sign reads:

JAMES CRAIG
JEWELLER
Engraving
Watch-Making
Done in the best manner

See? No cars.

No electricity.

There are actors.
They wear old clothes.

They wear coats.

They wear hats.

11

We can talk to them.

They teach us
about America.

We learn about the
start of our country.

They do the same things that people did 200 years ago.

They make the things they use.

Women spin yarn.

They sew.

15

A man makes boots.

He is a shoemaker.

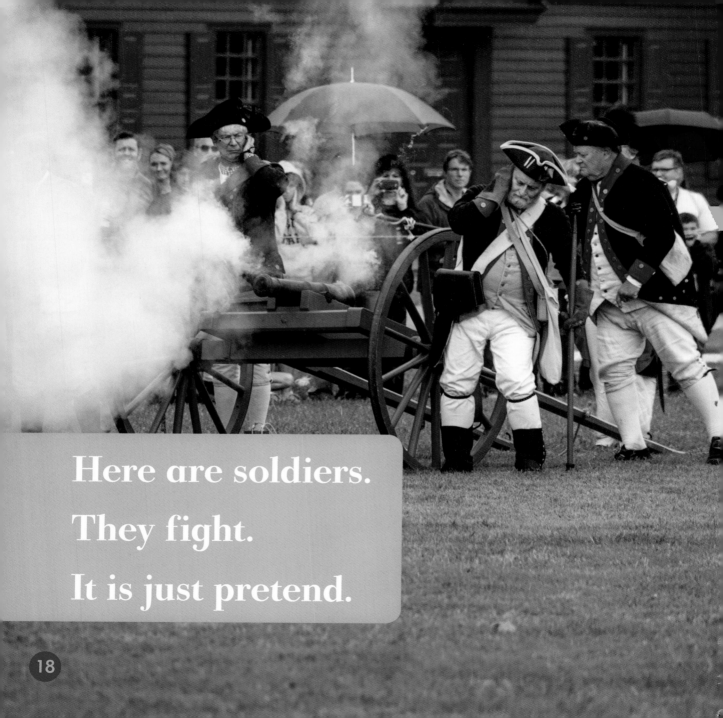

Here are soldiers.
They fight.
It is just pretend.

We can roll
a hoop. Fun!

hoop ·····▶

19

We love history!

Exploring Colonial Williamsburg

Governor's Palace

shoemaker

gunsmith

weaver

Picture Glossary

colonial
Relating to the original 13 colonies that formed the United States.

Williamsburg
A city in Virginia.

hoop
A toy in a game in which a hoop is rolled with a stick across the ground.

yarn
A fiber, like cotton or wool, made into a long thread for knitting, weaving, or sewing.

Index

To Learn More

Learning more is as easy as 1, 2, 3.

1) Go to www.factsurfer.com

2) Enter "ColonialWilliamsburg" into the search box.

3) Click the "Surf" button to see a list of websites.

With factsurfer.com, finding more information is just a click away.

24